Brown Bear and Red Goose have two children, a gosling named Charity and a cub named John. They all believe in God.

God Is All-Knowing
2013

ISBN-13: 978-1482375800

ISBN-10: 148237580X

God Is All-Knowing

The Attributes of God for Children

Charity and John came noisily down the stairs to find Papa. "Mama's going to buy us something good to eat at the store," they said. "But it's a secret!"

"How exciting!" said Papa. "I wonder what it is?"

"Do you think God knows what it is?" asked Charity.

"Let's see what the Bible has to say about that," said Papa. He took his Bible and began to read,

"Oh Lord, you have searched me and known me! You know when I sit down and when I get up . . . and know all about what I do. Even before I say a word, oh Lord, You know all about it" (Psalm 139.1–4).

"I'll bet God knows what Mama is going to buy!" said John.

"That's what the Bible says," said Papa. "God knows everything. So we can't keep any secrets from God."

"Does God know everything?" said Charity. "He must be very smart!"

"Yes," said Papa. "Just think how smart God is! All we know is a tiny, little part of everything, but God knows it all!

"He knows everything that has ever happened anywhere in the world, He knows everything that is happening right now, even on the farthest stars, and He knows everything that is going to happen, right down to the smallest thing. And He never makes any mistakes!"

"So God *does* know what Mama is going to buy!" said John.

"That's right," said Papa. "God knows everything we will do."

"But suppose Mama changes her mind," said Charity. "Then God would be wrong."

"No," Papa explained, "If Mama were to change her mind, then God would have known that instead. Whatever Mama would do, God would know about it before. It's impossible for Him to make a mistake."

"But if God already knows what Mama will do and it's impossible for Him to make a mistake, then can Mama really change her mind?" Charity insisted. "Doesn't she have to do what God knows she will do?"

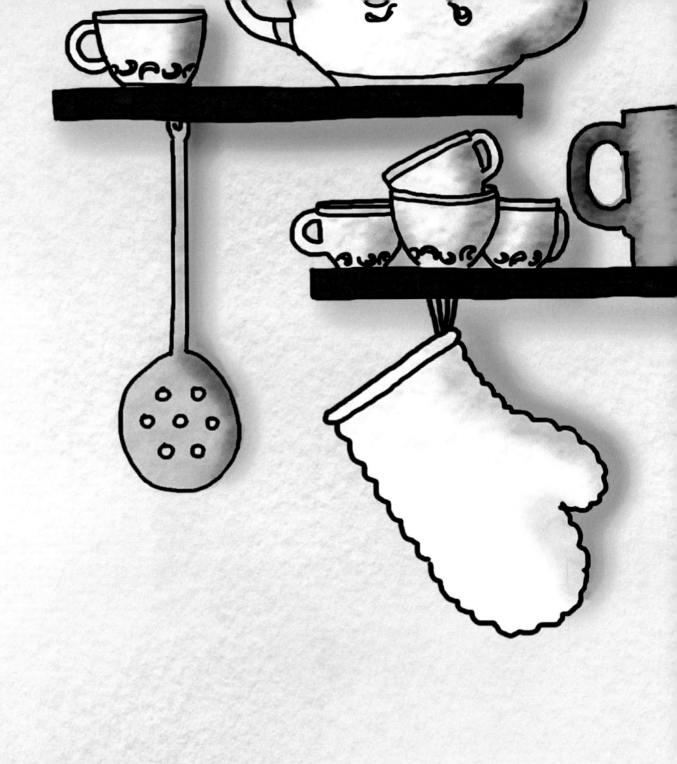

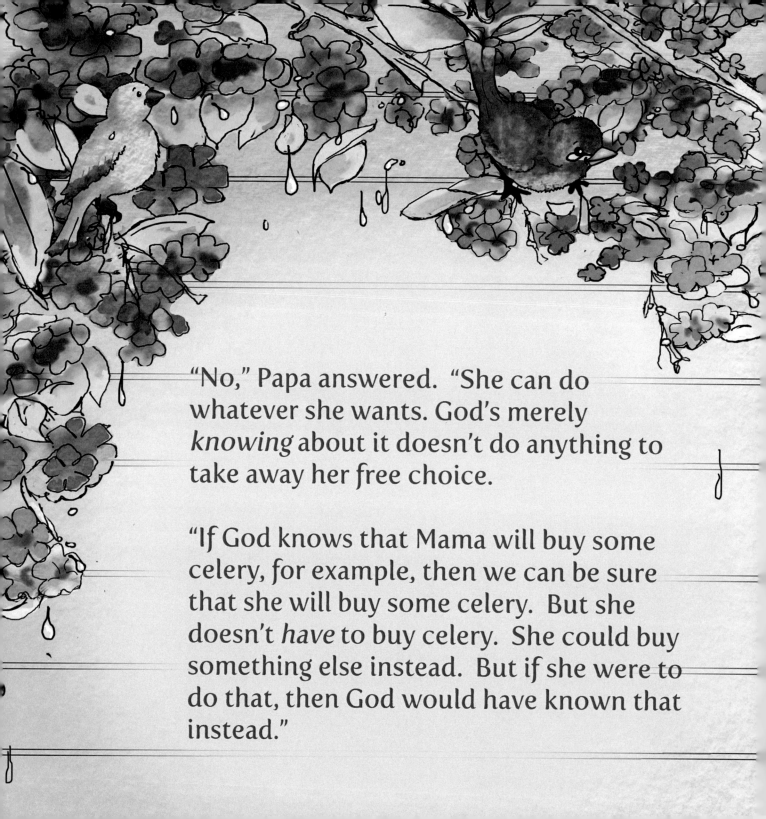

"No," Papa answered. "She can do whatever she wants. God's merely *knowing* about it doesn't do anything to take away her free choice.

"If God knows that Mama will buy some celery, for example, then we can be sure that she will buy some celery. But she doesn't *have* to buy celery. She could buy something else instead. But if she were to do that, then God would have known that instead."

"I hope she doesn't buy us some celery," grumped John.

"Don't worry," Papa laughed. "Even I know enough to be sure she won't do that!"

"Why is it important for us that God is all-knowing?" Papa asked.

"Because we can pray to Him!" said John.

"Very good, John," said Papa. "God says He will lead us through life if we trust in Him. It's easier to trust God and ask Him to lead us when we remember that He knows everything and never makes a mistake."

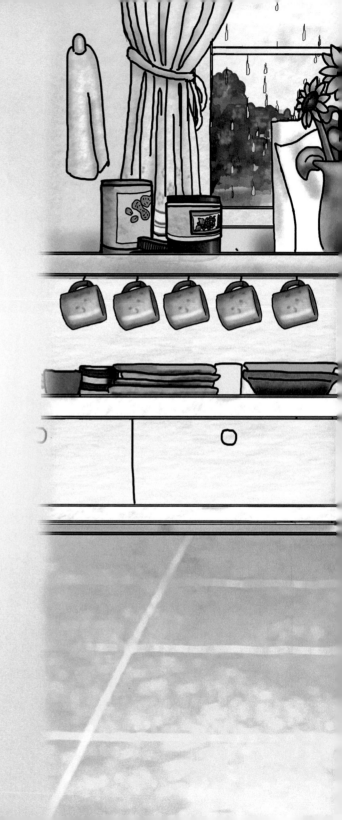

"What else?" Papa asked.

"Don't keep secrets from God?" said Charity.

"That's right!" Papa said. "When you do something wrong, don't try to hide it from God. He knows about it, and He still loves you. So ask Him to forgive you and help you to do better next time."

At that moment Mama walked in, carrying her shopping bag. "What did you buy? What did you buy?" cried Charity and John excitedly.

"Guess!" said Mama with a smile. "Celery!" said John. "Pears!" said Charity.

FAITH HOPE LOVE

"No," Mama replied, reaching into her bag. "Fresh strawberries, waffles, and cream! Surprised?"

"Yeah!" said Charity and John with delight. "But God knew it all along!"

Memory Verse:
"Even before I say a word, oh
Lord, You know all about it."
– Psalm 139:4

Books in the "What is God Like?" series

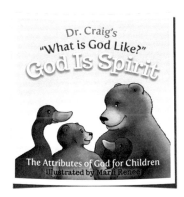

I. God is Spirit

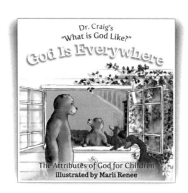

II. God is Everywhere

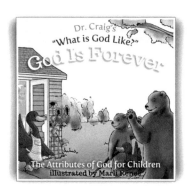

III. God is Forever

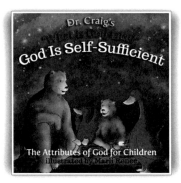

IV. God is Self-Sufficient

V. God is All-Knowing

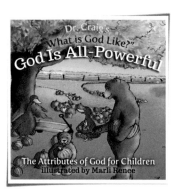

VI. God is All-Powerful

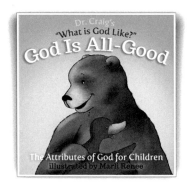

VII. God is All-Good

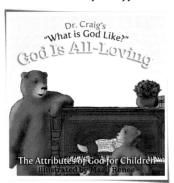

VIII. God is All-Loving

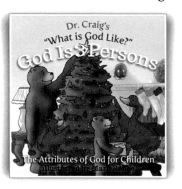

IX. God is Three Persons

X. The Greatness of God

"In these pages, you'll learn the most compelling arguments in favor of Christianity. You'll discover that *On Guard* is solidly factual, winsomely personal, consistently practical, and ultimately convincing in its presentation of the case for Christianity."

- Lee Strobel, former skeptic and author of *The Case for Christ* and *The Case for the Real Jesus*

ON GUARD

Defending Your Faith with Reason and Precision

WILLIAM LANE CRAIG

BEST-SELLING AUTHOR OF *REASONABLE FAITH*

On Guard and *On Guard Study Guide* are available at www.onguardbook.com

Made in the USA
San Bernardino, CA
10 July 2015